Our GREEN EARTH

FRIENDS IN THE WILD

Anne Flounders

RED CHAIR
•PRESS•

Please visit our website at **www.redchairpress.com**.
Find a free catalog of all our high-quality products for young readers.

Friends in the Wild

Publisher's Cataloging-In-Publication Data
(Prepared by The Donohue Group, Inc.)

Flounders, Anne.

Friends in the wild / Anne Flounders.
p. : ill., maps ; cm. -- (Our green Earth)
Summary: Did you know that the grass, trees, and dirt are the habitats or natural homes for insects, birds, and other animals? Learn why biodiversity is important, how the natural homes of various animals are being threatened, and what you can do to preserve and protect our natural environment. Includes step-by-step ideas for taking action, different points of view, an up-close look at relevant careers, and more.
Includes bibliographical references and index.
ISBN: 978-1-939656-41-4 (lib. binding/hardcover)
ISBN: 978-1-939656-29-2 (pbk.)
ISBN: 978-1-939656-48-3 (eBook)
1. Habitat (Ecology)--Juvenile literature. 2. Biodiversity--Juvenile literature. 3. Environmental protection--Juvenile literature. 4. Habitat (Ecology) 5. Biodiversity. 6. Environmental protection. I. Title.
QH541.14 .F56 2014

577   2013937160

Photo credits: Cover, title page, p. 5, 6, 7, 8, 9, 10, 11, 12, 13, 14, 15, 16, 17, 18, 19, 20, 22, 24, 26: Shutterstock; p. 4: © Francois Gohier, VWPics, Alamy; p. 6, 21, 25: Dreamstime; p. 23: Dawn Blake; p. 27: Richard Hutchings; p. 28: Anne Flounders; p.32: © Hildi Todrin, Crane Song Photography

This series first published by:
Red Chair Press LLC   PO Box 333   South Egremont, MA 01258-0333

Printed in the United States of America

1 2 3 4 5 18 17 16 15 14

MIX
Paper from
responsible sources
FSC
www.fsc.org   FSC® C002589

Table of Contents

CHAPTER ONE

Animals Matter

There are all kinds of animals in the world. Some are pretty amazing, like the blue whale. The world's largest animal, the blue whale can send messages to other whales more than a thousand miles away. Some animals seem ordinary. Think of the squirrel that hops through your yard. And some seem kind of yucky, like the dung beetle. It spends most of its life eating and hanging out in other animals' waste! But the fact is that every animal is important. Each animal is part of the web of life on Earth.

A natural variety of plant and animal life is called **biodiversity**. Biodiversity is important for a healthy planet.

Animals, including birds, fish, and insects, live just about everywhere on Earth. The place where an animal lives is called its **habitat**. A habitat is where an animal finds what it needs to survive. It finds food and a home. It can raise its young in its habitat. There are many kinds of habitats. Here are just a few examples.

Trees are a habitat for monkeys.

Grasslands are a habitat for bison.

Oceans are a habitat for whales.

Deserts are a habitat for lizards.

Many animals and plants live together in a certain place. That group, whether large or small, is called an **ecosystem**. An ecosystem helps living things survive together. Animals depend on their ecosystem and one another. People can help animals by protecting habitats and ecosystems.

Ponds are a habitat for turtles.

Tundras are a habitat for arctic foxes.

DID YOU KNOW?

There are about 8.7 million species of animals on Earth. About 6.5 million species live on land and 2.2 million live in the sea. But scientists say there are also thousands of species we don't know about.

Source: Science Daily

Explore an Ecosystem

Yellowstone National Park in Wyoming is an ecosystem. Yellowstone is home to 67 **species** of mammals, including bears, bison, deer, and wolves. About 148 species of birds make their nests in Yellowstone's trees. There are 16 species of fish living in the lakes, ponds, and rivers of Yellowstone, along with four species of amphibians. There are also many types of grasses, plants, and trees in the park. [1]

Yellowstone became a national park in 1872. But for many years before that, large populations of gray wolves had lived in the area. In the early part of the 20th century, people hunted gray wolves. By the 1930s, the gray wolf was almost **extinct**, meaning they were close to disappearing forever.

Gray wolves have no natural predators in Yellowstone's ecosystem.

[1] Source: National Park Service

The gray wolf was an important part of the Yellowstone ecosystem. The wolf is at the top of Yellowstone's food chain. That means the wolf had no **predators**, or animals who wanted to eat it. When the wolf's numbers fell, the populations of animals that the wolf had hunted began to rise. The numbers of elk, sheep, deer, and coyotes in the park soared. They needed to eat. So the numbers of grasses, plants, and small animals that they ate began to dwindle.

Beaver populations are back up in Yellowstone with the reintroduction of the gray wolf.

The animal activity that supported plants was affected. For example, after the wolf was taken away, elk began to roam nearer to willows by the riverbanks. They reduced the willow populations there. But the beavers had depended on the willows to live. They used them to build dams and create a habitat that helped them survive. Fewer willows meant a changed riverbank. The plants that had grown there and the animals that had thrived there could no longer survive. The ecosystem was thrown out of balance when the wolf was taken out.

People realized that the wolf mattered. Scientists and rangers moved some gray wolves from Canada to the park in 1995. Now the gray wolf population is rising again. The ecosystem is slowly moving back into balance.

The B-Team: Bats, Bees, Birds, Butterflies

Animals play important roles in every ecosystem. The help one another survive. They help plants grow. They even help people.

Bats, bees, birds, and butterflies are busy animals. They **pollinate** most of the plants on earth. They spread pollen from plant to plant. This allows plants to grow. The B-team pollinates 90 percent of all flowering plants and 75 percent of the world's main crops. Without bats, bees, birds, and butterflies, we would not have fruits or vegetables to eat.

Birds help protect the environment in many ways. They spread seeds for trees and plants. They eat bugs that could destroy plants, trees, and crops.

Birds help scientists understand the overall health of the environment. For example, a bird called the roseate spoonbill lives in the Florida Everglades. Roseate spoonbills, like other animals, are part of a food chain.

DID YOU KNOW?

Birds called vultures are a natural "clean-up crew." They eat dead animals. Removing dead animals from the open environment is healthier for people and other animals.

The birds eat fish. Fish survive by eating plants in the water. The plants depend on clean water to grow. Scientists saw that there were fewer roseate spoonbills in the Everglades. That led them to find that there were fewer fish, too. Scientists knew that there was a problem in the environment. Having such information is the first step toward finding a solution.

Our Earth needs biodiversity. All life on Earth has a role to play in helping others to survive. If one species is removed, it has a ripple effect. Other animals or plants suffer and could even go extinct, or disappear forever.

Animals have naturally faced extinction throughout time. Dinosaurs are a familiar example of a thriving species that is now extinct. But today, people's actions are causing animals and plants to face extinction at a faster rate than ever. Habitat loss, pollution, and climate change are just three big problems animals in the wild are facing. Scientists believe about one third of all known species may face extinction if people do not act. The consequences for the Earth could be enormous.

Only 30 Amur leopards are thought to exist in the wild.

CHAPTER TWO

Animals in the Wild

Polar bears have a problem. Their habitat is sea ice. Living on the ice allows them to easily catch seal, their main prey. But the polar bears' habitat is disappearing. Climate change has caused sea ice to melt.[2]

The polar bears' problem has been caused by humans. In fact, most of the survival issues among animals today are the result of human activity. But humans can also fix the problems.

Loss of sea ice means polar bears cannot hunt for food much of the year.

[2] Source: World Wildlife Federation

How does human activity lead to habitat loss? Here are a few examples of ways people change or destroy an animal's habitat.

- Burning fossil fuels, such as oil, coal, and natural gas. These release carbon dioxide in the atmosphere. Too much carbon dioxide builds up in the atmosphere. That leads to global warming and climate change. Climate change can mean more droughts, flooding, warmer water, and melting ice.

- Cutting down trees and forests for building or for agriculture.

- Polluting waterways.

- Introducing new species that do not belong in a habitat. These are called invasive species.

- Building dams to change waterways.

Many species are in danger due to deforestation.

An Unwelcome Neighbor

One example of an invasive species is a rodent called the nutria. This animal has caused great harm to the wetlands ecosystem.

The nutria was introduced to the United States from South America in the 1930s. It was brought here for its fur. Today, the nutria lives in wetlands near the United States' coastal areas. Wetlands rely on plants and trees to keep the habitat stable for birds and other wildlife that live there. But nutria eat and dig around those plants, which destroys the plants. That causes the soil to break up and wash away. Many wetlands have become open water because of the nutria. Loss of this land means more flooding in the surrounding areas. Nutria have also caused the population of native muskrats to decline.

Source: Washington Invasive Species Council

People will always need to build and do business. But more people are learning how habitat loss leads to problems in delicate ecosystems. More people are trying to change the way they treat the Earth so that we can preserve habitats. Even the way cities and towns grow can lead to habitat loss. Instead of building in fields and forests, some cities are making their existing neighborhoods more liveable. Warehouses and older buildings are being turned into housing and shops. This brings more people back into the existing city and preserves natural areas.

Helping Animals

Animals have many friends. Every day, people work hard to help animals and their habitats through **conservation**. Conservation is preserving and caring for the environment.

One way people help animals is by conserving habitats. Laws are made to protect the land where animals thrive. National parks, forests, and wildlife refuges are protected by the United States government. In these areas, animals live in their natural habitats. Laws protect habitats in areas where people build roads, homes, and businesses. Laws also prevent certain plants and animals from being introduced in places where they would cause problems.

Let's meet some animals in the wild who are being helped by people.

Sea Turtle – Sea turtles have lived for millions of years. But now they are in trouble. One problem they face is electric lights. Sea turtles lay their eggs on the beach. Baby turtles must move from the beach to the ocean at night. The turtles rely on the moonlight to help them find the ocean. If they see light from the other side of the beach, they get confused and head toward that light. If they do not reach the ocean, they cannot survive. People living near beaches are learning to change the way they use lights at night so they can help sea turtles.

Koala – Koalas live only in Australia. Koalas are picky eaters. They eat the leaves of one kind of tree. Climate change has affected the trees that koalas eat. They have less food. Another problem facing koalas is habitat fragmentation, or breaking up of their habitat. People have built roads that run through the areas where koalas live. They

must cross busy streets to find new trees. They may be struck by cars or attacked by dogs. People are helping koalas by planting trees, keeping dogs inside at night, and posting signs warning drivers about koalas.

Salmon – Pacific salmon used to number in the millions. They are born in fresh water rivers of the American northwest. They then swim to the Pacific Ocean where they grow. Later, they return to their river to lay their eggs. But pollution and dams on rivers have created problems for salmon. People are helping salmon in different ways.

They set up hatcheries where salmon can be hatched in good conditions. And 'fish ladders' help salmon make their way safely around dams.

Jaguar – Jaguars are large cats that live in Central and South America. Their main habitat is tropical forests and other wet, grassy areas. Jaguars were once much prized for their fur. Many were killed for their spotted coats. Hunting jaguar is no longer legal, but jaguars still face many problems. They have lost much of their habitat to logging, agriculture, and building. Habitat loss also means fewer animals for the jaguar to prey upon. So jaguars often eat livestock from ranches. This angers ranchers, who kill jaguars to protect their livestock. People are working with ranchers to come up with better solutions to protect both jaguars and livestock. Wildlife preserves have been set up so jaguars can roam freely in their natural habitat. Scientists are studying where jaguars live and how they move from place to place. The information will help them learn how to protect jaguars.

Giant Panda – The giant panda lives in China. It has lost much of its habitat. One reason is that people are moving into the land where pandas live and eat. They remove bamboo and other plants the panda needs. Conservationists have been working with the government in China to set aside more land for the panda's habitat. The panda's numbers may be slowly going up. But for now, they are still endangered.

Brown Pelican – The brown pelican lives along the Gulf coast of the United States. The bird was an endangered species until recently. In 2009, its numbers had gone up so much that it was removed from the Endangered Species list. But in 2010, a major oil spill occurred in the Gulf of Mexico. Many wondered if the pelicans could survive the damage to their habitat. People are working to clean up the oil from the spill. It is a long process. Scientists are also watching the pelican population. Now pelicans are nesting again.

DID YOU KNOW?
More than 1,300 animals and plants in the United States are considered threatened or endangered. That means they could become extinct if we do not act.

CHAPTER THREE

Animals in Your Backyard

Kids may wonder: Is there anything I can do to help animals? If I live in Vermont, can I help jaguars in South America? If I live in Kansas, can I help koalas in Australia?

The answer is *yes*. Everyone is part of the enormous ecosystem of Earth. Just as taking one animal out of a food web effects the entire web, taking care of the earth where we live can help the whole planet.

We can all help the ecosystem of our own backyards.

Plants and Animals

Trees, grasses, and flowers all depend on animals to grow. In turn, animals need trees and plants for food and shelter. And all these species work together to ensure that people have clean air and clean water.

Japanese Knotweed crowds out native plants.

Over the past century, development has taken over much of the land. Houses and buildings stand where wild spaces once stood. Changes such as these cause problems in our ecosystems. For example, plants that don't belong in an area may have been placed there by well-meaning gardeners. But non-native plants may not offer the proper food to native species. And they may become invasive species, crowding out native plants.

People can help by planting more trees, shrubs, grasses, and flowering plants that belong in the area. These provide habitats for animals.

There are many things people can do to help keep animals' habitats healthy and safe for many years.

Use less plastic. Use reusable drinking bottles and shopping bags instead of plastic, for example.

Eat less meat. One meat-free day a week can help reduce the amount of land needed for ranches that produce meat.

Don't litter. Pick up litter when you see it.

Learn everything you can about your local ecosystems. The more people know, the more valuable it becomes to them. Spend time outdoors. Observe nature. Find out about the health of the water, land, and species in your area.

Plant trees and flower gardens. Give animals in your area places to live and to eat.

Don't use chemical fertilizers. Chemicals get into the water system. They can be harmful to animals in and around the water. Use natural fertilizers to feed a lawn or garden.

COLLEGE TO CAREER

Do you think you might be interested in a career that helps animals in the wild?

Here are just a few of the jobs you could do.

Aquatic Ecologist	*Wildlife Biologist*
Conservation Scientist	*Park Ranger*
Veterinarian	*Wildlife Refuge Specialist*

As a wildlife biologist for the Hoopa Valley Tribe in California, Dawn Blake helps create safe habitat corridors in the tribe's timber program. "Our tribe is very aware of wildlife and we are trying to measure the effectiveness of our efforts by tracking animals such as the pileated woodpecker," says Dawn. "The field trips and hands-on experiences I had at Humboldt State University led me to this field. My instructors were passionate about wildlife. That made me value what I was learning."

DAWN BLAKE

People, Pets, and Nature

Pets live the easy life. Dogs and cats curl up in a sunny spot on the living-room floor. Hamsters and gerbils enjoy a good run on their wheels. Pets are good company for their owners. They don't have to look for food in the wild. Food and water are given to pets by owners.

Most pet cats are happiest living indoors.

The way we care for pets can affect animals in the wild. Dogs need to go outside to exercise and use "nature's bathroom." Pet cats do best living inside. Cats who roam outside tend to kill birds. One study has shown that cats living outside kill nearly 3.5 billion birds per year in the United States. They also kill almost 20.7 billion small animals, such as mice and rabbits.[3]

People should choose pets they know they can care for. Releasing a pet into the wild can cause harm to the ecosystem. It can also harm or kill the released pet. Pet fish, snakes, rodents, or other small animals put into the wild become invasive species. In Florida, pythons released into the Everglades have become a problem. They compete with native species for food and space. The snakes are also eating endangered native species, such as the wood rat and the wood stork.

Finally, no one should capture a wild animal to keep as a pet. Leave animals in their own habitats. It is the best way for them to survive.

[3] Source: *Nature Communications* Journal

FACE OFF: Cats in the Wild: Trap, Neuter, Return?

It's a fact: Tens of millions of homeless cats roam around the United States.

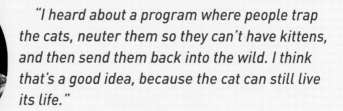

"I heard about a program where people trap the cats, neuter them so they can't have kittens, and then send them back into the wild. I think that's a good idea, because the cat can still live its life."

Trap-Neuter-Return (TNR) is one strategy some communities use to manage homeless, or **feral**, cats. These cats often cannot learn to live with people after living their lives in the open. TNR does allow the cats to live. It is considered humane, or kind, to the cats. Spaying or neutering a homeless cat is healthier for the animal. It allows them to gain weight and live longer lives. Most important, they cannot have more kittens. However, feral cats face their own dangers out in the wild. They are often killed by cars, disease, predators, or extreme hot or cold.

"I don't think homeless cats should be returned to the streets. They kill so many birds! Can't people give the cats homes?"

In some cases, homeless cats can find homes after they are trapped. Some find "jobs" as mouse-catchers for farmers. But feral, or wild, cats kill billions of birds and other small animals each year. Most of the homeless cats can never learn to live with people.

What do you think?

Backyard Biodiversity

The space around one's home or school is an ecosystem. Animals live there. Birds and insects may be the most common species people see every day. But chances are that no matter where a person lives, there is a huge variety of animals and plants. Many depend on each other to survive.

People help animals by studying them. Scientists study animals in their natural habitats. If they notice something unusual, such as a decline in numbers, they can investigate and figure out what the problem might be. They share the information with others who can help solve the problem.

Anybody can act like a scientist in their own backyard or neighborhood. Take a good look around at different times of day. What animals do you see or hear? Do you see any other clues that animals have been around? For example, are there holes? Tracks? Find out what species are native to your

area. Do a little research to find out how healthy their populations are. Know who your friends in the wild are. Knowledge is a good way to begin to help animals.

BUILD A BIRD BATH

Invite animals into your yard at home or at school by creating a friendly habitat for them. Birds need fresh water. Here is how you can make a bird bath. You'll need:

- Terra cotta clay flower pots of various sizes
- Terra cotta clay dish (these are often sold with the flower pots)
- Ceramic glue
- A rock
- Optional: Paint

Here's what to do:

Step 1: Use two pots: one should be upside down and one placed on top of it, right-side up. The bottoms will be touching. Glue the bottoms together with ceramic glue. If you want to paint the pots, do so before gluing them.

Step 2: Attach the dish to the top of the base. Use ceramic glue to secure the center of the dish to the center of the base.

Step 3: Place a small rock in the center of the dish. This gives birds an extra space to land on.

Step 4: Place the bird bath in partial shade near a tree or shrub.

Step 5: Fill the dish with about 2.5 inches of clean water.

Step 6: Enjoy watching the birds!

Step 7: Be sure to keep the bird bath filled with clean water.

On The Job

Name: Maggie Howell

Job: Executive Director, Wolf Conservation Center, South Salem, NY

What is the Wolf Conservation Center?

Maggie Howell: We're a blend of education and recovery. Zephyr, Alawa, and Atka are our ambassador wolves. Through these wolves, we open the door to understanding the importance of their wild kin. We have these guys teaching onsite, we have one wolf that travels, and we have eight webcams that help us reach a global audience. We participate in the recovery of two critically endangered wolf species. One is the Mexican gray wolf. The other is the red wolf. Both are extremely rare. As a participant in the recovery, we house them, we have captive breeding, and we suggest which of these wolves should be released. Two of our Mexican gray wolves were released into the wilds of Arizona.

What are some successes you have had in your work?

MH: One of the things we're so proud of is releasing those two wolves back into the wild. It's amazing to think these were two animals we were tasked with taking care of; we're connected to them. They live here in New York, and then they're wild wolves in Arizona! That was pretty incredible.

Are you hands-on with the wolves?

MH: I clean and pick up poop. I go in the fencing frequently enough to keep up my relationship with the wolves. I'm one of Atka's handlers. I'm lucky to have that opportunity because I was not here to help raise Atka. His three other handlers were all here to raise him. But I met him at a point when he was still open to new friends.

So when we go to a school or other offsite visit, normally I do the talking. But if we have to switch things around, I can handle Atka as well.

What do you enjoy most about your work?

MH: What I enjoy most is being in this setting. No complaints! I feel like I'm leaving a mark. That's something I try to encourage in my daughter. She wants to open up a snake conservation center! I tell her, you can do whatever you want; I hope that whatever you do, you feel like you're making an impact.

Why is wolf conservation so important?

MH: The wolf is what we call a keystone species, which means they are an important part of nature's puzzle. If the wolf is in place it can hold everything in balance. It's going keep the habitat healthy, trees and plants. And if the trees and plants are healthy, it provides food and shelter for other animals. In Yellowstone park, wolves were missing for 70 years until the mid-1990s when they were reintroduced. Once they were reintroduced, they found that wolves had an impact on their prey, which was the elk. Fewer elk weren't eating so many trees and plants, so the trees and plants grew back. Then because they touched the habitat, they touched all sorts of different creatures: beavers, river otters, song birds, moose, and even butterflies benefited by wolves being back. The wolf was the glue, that piece that held everything in a healthy balance.

What's the greatest threat to wolves?

MH: Wolves need a lot of land, so habitat destruction has a big impact on wolf survival. If we can keep certain populations of wolves safe in our country, not only is it good for wolves, but it keeps the habitat they need safe as well.

Check it out: nywolf.org

Glossary

biodiversity — the variety of plant and animal life in our world or in a habitat

conservation — protecting or restoring something in the environment

ecosystem — a system made up of living things interacting with their environment

extinct — no longer in existence

feral — to be similar to a wild animal; not domesticated or ready to live with humans

habitat — the natural home of a plant, animal, or organism

pollinate — to carry and deposit pollen from one plant to another

predators — animals that prey, or hunt, other animals in nature

species — a group of living things that share common features or traits

For More Information

Books

Ballard, Carol. *Watching Wildlife: Animal Habitats.* Heinemann-Raintree, 2009.

Bredeson, Carmen. *Weird But True Animal Homes.* Enslow, 2011.

Web Sites

Go Wild (World Wildlife Fund): *Learn about protecting the natural world.*
http://gowild.wwf.org.uk/

National Wildlife Federation Kids: *Games, activities, and wildlife blogs.*
http://www.nwf.org/kids.aspx

Wildlife Careers: *The staff at the National Zoo in Washington, D.C., tell how to prepare now for a career helping animals.*
http://nationalzoo.si.edu/education/wildlifecareers/default.cfm

All web addresses (URLs) have been reviewed carefully by our editors. Web sites change, however, and we cannot guarantee that a site's future contents will continue to meet our high standards of quality and educational value.

INDEX

About the Author

Anne Flounders has lots of on-the-job experience writing for kids and teens. She has written and edited magazines, nonfiction books, teachers' guides, reader's theater plays, and web content. She has also recorded narration for audio- and ebooks. Anne protects our green Earth with her husband and son in Connecticut.